5 SECRETS TO PODCASTING!

An introductory guide to
Monetizing Podcasts and
how to succeed at it

By Tom Cavallaro

- Founder of Internet Radio Academy -

A Publication of

CAVALLARO

CAVALLARO

Authored By Thomas J. Cavallaro Jr.

illustrations By Thomas J.Cavallaro Jr

Cover By: Angie English
Frist Edition - Copyright 2014

THANKS

I dedicate this book to my family. To my wife Jennifer and Daughter Gabriella, who sacrificed for me being away from home for 10-12 hours a day at the office, To my Mother who always encouraged and supported me, and my brother who has been my friend, supporter, sounding board, and confidant. I love appreciate you all very much.

In addition my thanks to all the people I have met in my 26 years in the media industry, for helping me learn. To each of my Bosses and Co-workers for educating me, making me better and pushing me to excel all a long my way... I have been fortunate to know you!

I thank you for buying this book.

Helping others grow is one if the best feelings there is.

Thank you all. Tom

TABLE OF CONTENTS

INTRODUCTION

BY A FORMER DIRECTOR PROGRAMMING & SALES AT CBS RADIO - NEW YORK

Back in 2007, while working at CBS Radio I was given a fantastically amazing, once in a lifetime opportunity.

The awesome chance to be creative in a Pioneering area of the Radio industry, Digital Online Radio, AKA Streaming Radio. I will never forget those who gave me this break and their trust.

Like for many of you reading this, there was so much to do, to learn and figure out. Along with this opportunity came what I thought of at the time was the biggest challenge, being given ZERO BUDGET. Yes you read that correctly.

I was given Zero, Nada, Nothing to start with, except a promise that if I could presell, I would get my own studio, and an experienced and capable radio partner to work with on studio operation production of the shows, and together we would build out the station.

Looking back now the Zero budget was simply a speed bump.

CAVALLARO

INTRODUCTION

So I was in a situation you might very well be in, of having zero dollars to work with, and with added pressures paying your personal expenses to live. My added pressure was levels of corporate bureaucracies looming over me, and having to wade through layers for approvals on each and every move I made.

This was in a few words, Not Easy, and a very frustrating time for me. I understood and respected the experience and dedication of the people around me. I eventually came to the realization of understanding that this was a new area of Radio for the company. I tried and realized that some diplomacy was a key in dealing with the Old Guard for support on something they did not like for the industry they grew up in, protected, and loved so much.

Looking back there was so many changes happening not only in the company, with its massive layoffs, and format changes of historic forty plus year old stations, but the economy was in free fall, it was a very scary time in the world as you well know.

I saw the future back then, and I would let nothing stop me... There actually became a time when I stopped asking and started just taking massive actions and doing, apologizing rather that asking... it was at huge risks and yes I did piss people off quite well I must say. Through it all I must say I cherish the memories of this time, it was so much fun! Especially when I made it all happen!

CAVALLARO

INTRODUCTION

For The record please know the strategies we preach and teach have been developed through years of real world testing and rollout application in a corporate bureaucracy setting.

Even with these challenges was able to generate just under 1.7 million is sales year one. This was done with Zero Support and Budget by stacking revenues streams from outside sales teams, this on top of what I sold in-house, always making sure that audience directed to come back to us as the center core of our universe.

This eBook is an Introduction of Fundamentals to Monetization of Podcasts. You might consider hiring Tom Cavallaro for consultation, if in fact you find yourself in a hurried situation to reach you financial goals, Services available for publishers at all levels and status.

CAVALLARO

INTRODUCTION

This eBook is created for both the startup podcaster as well as the Seasoned podcaster alike. If you are advanced, not to worry we have made sure to have valuable and useful content here for you.

Some of our rules, never ever stop learning. Never interrupt someone who is telling us something we think we know everything about. For the simple reasons we might learn something new, remember something we had forgotten, or learn where we can be of assistance with sharing our knowledge.

At a minimum it's a review confirming and measuring what we know, which is always a win. it is also helpfully important to know that we are all on the same page.

What you will gain from this eBook...

- Look at the Past, Present and Future
- Discovery of your why
- Standard Expectations of Advertising Agencies and Advertisers
- Importance of Knowing who your audience is, and their wants
- Benefits of online Syndication
- How to package your product for sale to advertisers
- What Makes You Money
- Knowing we are here as a resource designed for you

CAVALLARO

INTRODUCTION

Today every major media company is scrambling to figure out how to serve and reach the new techno-hounds that everyone has become.

The Online and Mobile challenges are the same for all, it is truly a leveling playing field as long as you can see the road ahead.

Major media companies still have some advantage over you, however Its now slowly waning. It is proven with the right plan, dedication to quality production, determination, along with your ability, and with some guidance you can meet the grade.

Back in the mid 1990's while at a University Conference Bill Gates was asked by a student; What are you most afraid of? He replied, ***"Two Guys in A Garage!"***

The Independent show and stations, your advantage is the ability to move and make decisions quickly, follow trends, and have little, to no bureaucracy to manage or to get in your way.

It Is Our Goal and Honor to be of Trusted Service Helping You...

CHAPTER

1

PODCAST PIONEERING

Hello My Podcast Pioneer Friend!

Pioneer? Why Yes You Are a Pioneer! Yes, You are right Podcasting started in the late 1980's with services called Audioblogging. AB was very limited in audience, simply because of the number of users knowing of its existence, lack of... or lets say limited content, with most users stuck to a desk top PC, and no real bandwidth.

Then in 2004 the IPod hit the world, (*Thanks Steve!*) allowing for huge numbers of audio files storage in a tiny pocket size and mobile device.

One year later in 2005 the launch of ITunes and Podcasting took off like a preverbal rocket. ITunes provided a platform that was simple and easy. Publishers now had the ability to digitally feed, post and deliver content. Providing the audience users with cool audio files of all kinds of subject matter that they could subscribe to with the convenience of scheduled automation downloads, this changed everything...

It's still changing everything... and You are a Part of it!
10-Years gone by and the masses worldwide are still just learning about the existence, convenience, and amazing content of podcasts.

We Appreciate and Applaud You!

Tom Cavallaro - Founder

CHAPTER

1

PODCAST PIONEERING

Back in 2007 when I was working for the number one national revenue producing radio group, as an Executive Director Sales and Programming, Creating Digital Radio Stations and Verticals, while simultaneously working for number one Radio News Station in the USA, I saw a wave of change coming. It was 45 years of core services that were no longer going to be relevant to the 5-W's. "The I **want**, **what** I **want**, **when** I **want** it audience." Why did I believe this to be so? What happened?

So imagine now **your core audience service and draw** is traffic and weather. Traffic: Every 10 minutes on the 1's, every hour of every day, Weather: Every 4 minutes, every hour, around the clock... well its too bad for you because just about everyone today knows by simply looking at their hand held device, or now in Dash-screen what the weeks weather is, and more importantly what the traffic ahead is, also the best alternate route to circumvent the traffic. Over 45-Years It was great riding the wave! Revenues of 50 million now down to 30 million in just 7 years, Ouch! **No longer riding wave, now getting hit by it.**

Fact is this 5-W's audience of today simply can have **what they want, when they want it. You Need To Know it and Deliver it!**

CHAPTER

2

SECRET TO WHY?

Why, is something only you know. So why are you reading this?

Better question, why are You Podcasting? I am betting it is for the following reasons. You want to meet cool people, and want to help people even if its just making them smile, laugh and enjoy the time spent listening to your show. You want to be Famous, and you want to make money doing what you love to do.

I want you to know that all of these "whys" are achievable, and more than possible with your dedicated efforts to a long term plan, with short term goals. Put your plan to paper, think about goals, map them out, and the most important **Secret is to Take Massive Action!**

Do what you are most excited about first. These will be the easiest for you to accomplish. Use your gut instincts, intuition, and you will build momentum on each task like a freight train going down hill. Taking massive action once begun builds, and can become infectious excitement, where you get others on the train ride with you, to collectively reach the Why's you set for yourself.

Remember what appears as failures on tasks is simply learning. It is your investment in first hand knowledge. The gaining of first hand knowledge is never a failure. Own it and use each failed attempt to reach for the goal again. Taking one from Nike "***Just do it!***" but do it *Again Differently, and now you know WHY!*

CHAPTER

3

KNOWING YOUR AUDIENCE

One of Your Greatest Challenges Is Meeting Industry **Standards**

Advertising Agencies, and their Client Advertisers buy digital media inventory according to I.A.B. (*Internet Advertising Bureau)* standards, and these standards are based on Impressions (*the number of Ads seen or heard, and frequency of ads}*, GEO targeting (*Aka - Geography by Market and can be as local as Zip code*) and Demo (Aka – Audience *Demographics)* In addition to who your audience is, the percentages description of your audience, are they Male, Female, Age, Income, and lastly what are they interested in buying.

These standards can not be met by using services like survey monkey or even your own audience survey.

Arbitron, Nielsen, and Market Research Incorporated "MRI" are the standards of today under guidance of the IAB. This is a HUGE annual financial investment that prices out a majority of podcasters, online radio shows, stations, and many independent broadcast stations alike.

But worry not my friend, we provide an inexpensive one time fee industry standard solution, in addition we can bring high paying Advertising Agencies Clients, once audience data is compiled, and we can teach you how to use these tools, and audience data on your own to sell more advertisers and make more money...

CHAPTER

3

KNOWING YOUR AUDIENCE

One of Your Greatest Challenges Is Meeting Industry **Standards**

So far we have reviewed the **importance of knowing your audience and meeting the Industry Standards.** Meeting the standards will position your show so that Ad-agencies can buy your show, matching your show and audience to other shows and stations to complete the Buy. The Buy or campaign is the total reach of audience they need on the campaign rollout to deliver the projected ROI, return on investment.

A select number of markets and a total number of impressions required along with rate of Ads frequency per individual exposure is a predetermination, which is made based on a prior market test, which then becomes the model for the rolling out of an advertising campaign across all designated markets and media outlet shows, stations and podcast publishers like yours.

Also know that ad-agencies are pros at this and they are very much accountable to their client advertisers. You have the same challenge you are accountable to the ad-agencies and or advertisers and collectively must deliver a on predetermined ROI for the advertiser, especially If you expect to keep them as clients. A digital campaign usually includes a tracking code so agencies can see activity on a dashboard on their end. They are watching second by second to see if the stations/shows on the campaign are delivering the projected and required number of impressions and actions. Note If a show or station is failing to deliver they are usually contacted and receive a cancellation. Happens to biggest and best of them, guess how I know.

4

ONLINE & MOBILE AUDIENCE

NEXT TWO PAGES SHOULD **GET YOU EXCITED**
YOU DECIDED TO CREATE A PODCAST

According to 2012 study by PEW Institute The vast majority of Americans still report listening to AM/FM radio weekly. But, as many as **40% percent of Americans now listen to audio on digital devices, and that is projected to double by 2015**, while interest in traditional radio even the HD option is on the decline. One of the prime arenas for digital listening was the car, once the domain of AM/FM radio.

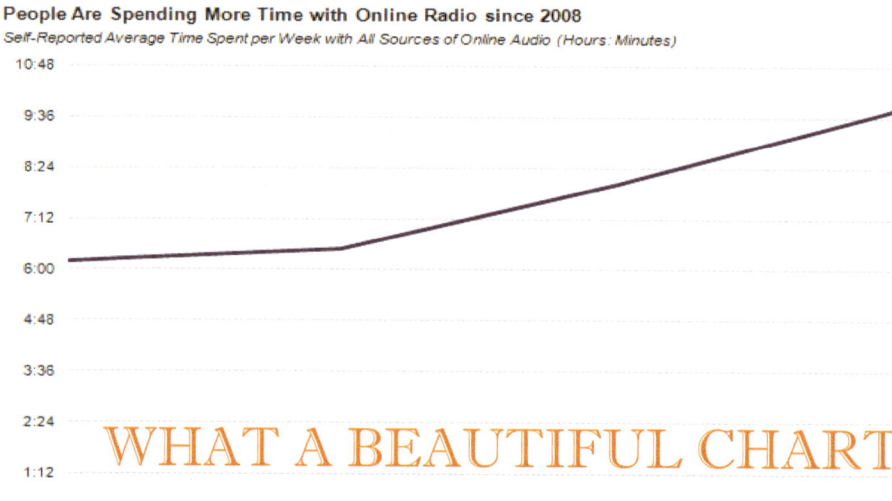

People Are Spending More Time with Online Radio since 2008
Self-Reported Average Time Spent per Week with All Sources of Online Audio (Hours: Minutes)

WHAT A BEAUTIFUL CHART

Source: Arbitron

PEW RESEARCH CENTER'S PROJECT FOR EXCELLENCE IN JOURNALISM
2012 STATE OF THE NEWS MEDIA

CHAPTER

4

ONLINE & MOBILE AUDIENCE

WHAT IS YOUR PLAN
TO **GET YOUR SHARE** OF THESE DOLLARS?

Online and Mobile Radio Expected to See Richest Revenue Gains

In Millions of Dollars

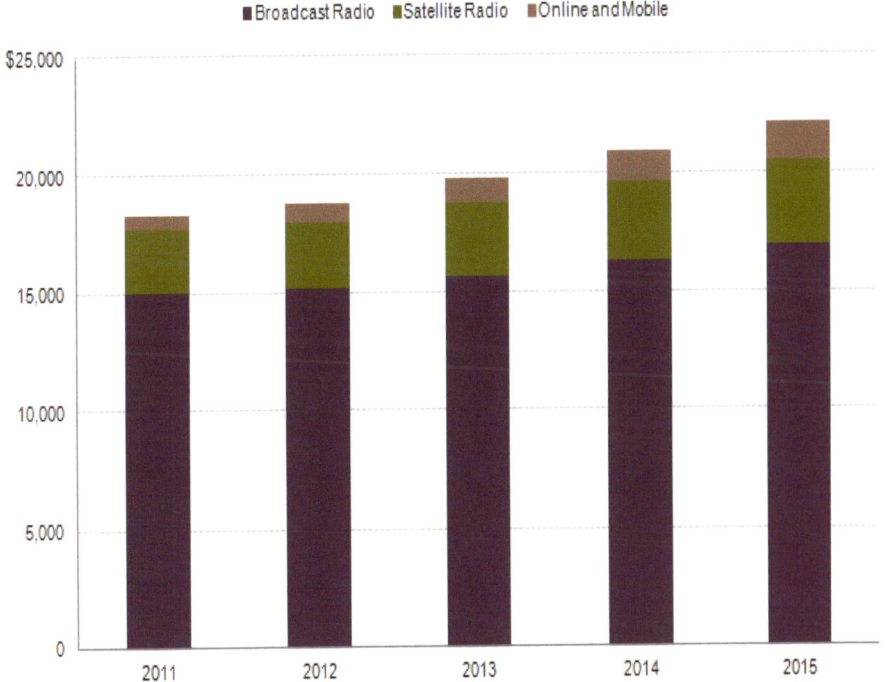

■ Broadcast Radio   ■ Satellite Radio   ■ Online and Mobile

Source: Veronis Suhler Stevenson Communications Industry Forecast 25th Edition, 2011 – 2015

5

SYNDICATION

As Chaucer said around year 1391, all roads lead to Rome. Simply be Rome. Make all roads lead to your show website, and or station website. Remember though to always **FEED the People what they want, what they cannot get anywhere else.**

Knowing how to syndicate your podcast is very important. It is the difference between a popular podcast that gets noticed, and builds subscribers or one that never gets off the ground.

The key is all about Syndicating Online From Your Position. **You Control The Size of Your World,** Be The Center of Your Universe and Make it Huge. Yes, it can be tedious work, and on top of everything else you must plan and do, there's a lot of time, and cash investment, but it is well worth your efforts.

Benefits: 1) Exposure to Directories Audience.
2) Backlinks to Your Show Website.
3) Improved Search Engine Rankings.

Today there is dozens and dozens of podcast directories, get on them. There's no need to recreate the wheel just roll it...

CHAPTER

5

SYNDICATION

BUILD YOUR AUDIENCE

AROUND YOU

CHAPTER

What Makes The Money

Your Show is a subscriber, credibility, and Traffic building tool...

With the right structure even a relatively small subscriber base can generate you six- figure incomes. You just need to put the puzzle together correctly. Of course Its not going to do it itself, you will need to be obsessed, which more than likely you already are, or you would not be spending your time reading this...

As mentioned typically brick and mortar advertisers buy media on a market by market basis, (GEO-targeted) where they can actually service consumers with their local stores.

Simple Monetization Examples:

So lets imagine you specialize your podcasts around home gardening. You make contact with your local gardening center and you offer a cross promotion sponsorship opportunity to the store owner or manger.

This would typically be for a private or small chain size business where decisions are made locally. You could offer an exclusive Title Sponsorship, Studio Title Sponsorship, or Segment Sponsorship to them for some cash and allow them to have rights to post your podcasts on their website as a services to their customers. You can go department by department covering each area, tie in and highlight their selected suppliers products.

We have done this similarly on an international level with the world Famous Dr. Neil De Grasse Tyson's show called "Star Talk Radio", we structured a Cross Podcast partnership deal with Discovery Magazine.

CHAPTER

6

BONUS

~~FIVE~~ 9 WAYS TO
MONETIZE YOUR PODCASTS

- **If You Got audience? We'll get you sponsors**

- **Go get your own sponsors**

- **Cross-promoting with Partner Sponsors for a Win-Win-Win**

- **Build a Network of programs sell advertising on and around it**

- **Use your show to promote Affiliate products or services**

- **Build your brand sell and leverage your own products or services**

- **Integrate sponsorship with the show's editorial/interviews**

- **Cliffhanger - Partial show free, full show paid**

- **Donations is bottom rung but look at Public Radio/TV it works**

"**You Control The Size Of Your World, Be The Center of Your Universe and Make it Huge.**"

Tom Cavallaro - Founder

WE ARE

HERE FOR YOU

Everyone needs some help from time to time. Some people want to do everything on their own, others want to be the Captain of the ship but don't want to build it.

Please know we and our scalable bundles of services are here for you no matter your chosen course...

Truly hope we have excited you and provided you with enough information for inspiration to build on your dreams. Now get on too the perspiration and make it so!

Interested in having MRI Audience Survey Data of Your Podcasts, Shows or Station?

Need Some One On One Help?

Need Advertising Sales Guidance Call Our Offices : **631-780-4607**

www.InternetRadioAcademy.com

CAVALLARO

Notes